ABC's

for All Ages

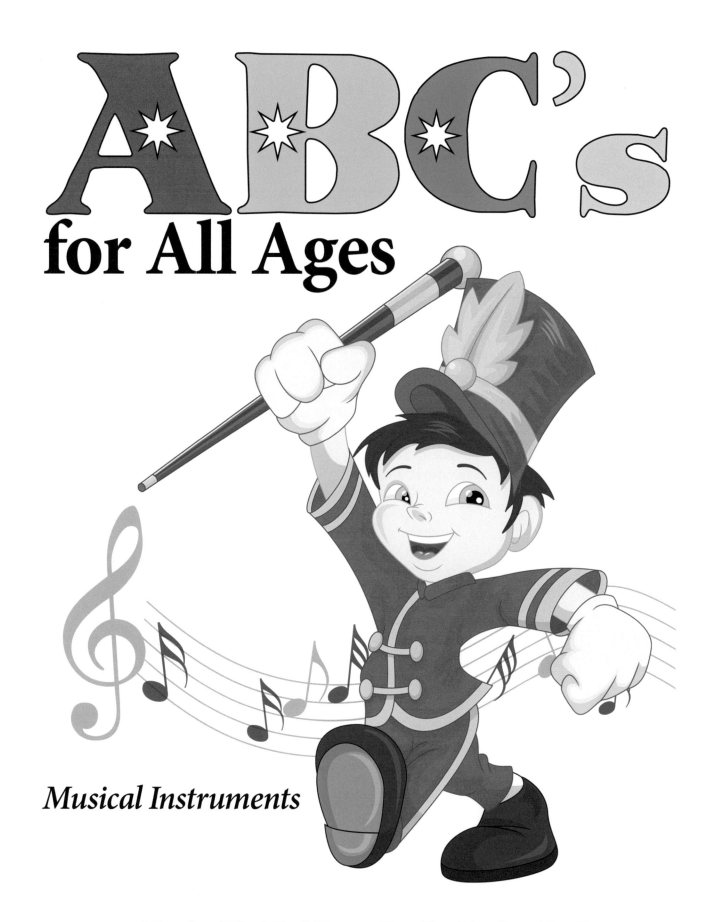

Musical Instruments

PATTY COPPER

Archway Publishing books may be ordered through booksellers or by contacting:

Archway Publishing
1663 Liberty Drive
Bloomington, IN 47403
www.archwaypublishing.com
1 (888) 242-5904

Because of the dynamic nature of the Internet, any web addresses or links contained in this book may have changed since publication and may no longer be valid. The views expressed in this work are solely those of the author and do not necessarily reflect the views of the publisher, and the publisher hereby disclaims any responsibility for them.

Any people depicted in stock imagery provided by Thinkstock are models, and such images are being used for illustrative purposes only.
Certain stock imagery © Thinkstock.

ISBN: 978-1-4808-5340-9 (sc)
ISBN: 978-1-4808-5341-6 (hc)
ISBN: 978-1-4808-5389-8 (e)

Print information available on the last page.

Archway Publishing rev. date: 10/19/2017

♪

To Mike and Doug

Thank you for changing
my life into music.

Please join me in keeping the rhythm
and beat to these musical instruments.

A is for **A**ccordion
a squeeze box they say

B is for **B**ass you
stand up to play

Cymbals go CRASH don't get in the way

D is for Drums they keep the beat

Euphoniums are really, really neat

French horns and Flutes
play in the band

All **G**uitars you
play with both hands

Harmonicas are small
they fit in your palm

I is for Instruments that can sooth and calm

Jamborees are like parties you can dance and sing

Keyboards can sound like anything

Lyres and Lutes are old – fashioned
like queens and kings

M is for **M**aracas that you shake, shake, shake

N is for the Noise that they make, make, make

Oboe is a funny word

A Piccolo sounds as
sweet as a bird

You play **Q**uints **5** at a time

Many Recorders start to rhyme

Saxophones are instruments you hear in jazz

Tubas, Trumpets, and Trombones
adds pizzazz

Ukuleles are
small you play on
the go

Violins and **V**iolas you play with a bow

Woodwinds
are sometimes
hard to blow

Xylophones you hit with mallets or sticks

Yodel is a song that you sing for kicks
Yodel - ay - ee - hoo

A Zither is an instrument that you pluck and pick

Pick up an instrument any night or day
And you will yell hip - hip hooray.

Patty Copper has been
a high school teacher for
twenty years. She lives in
Irmo, South Carolina, with
her husband, Mike. Patty has
a son and a grandson.

Printed in the United States
By Bookmasters